Everest

A PLAY BY
KAREN GLENN

READ180™

SCHOLASTIC INC.

New York Toronto London Auckland Sydney
Mexico City New Delhi Hong Kong

ILLUSTRATIONS BY

MATT COLLINS

DESTINATION: EVEREST was first published as "Terror on the Mountain" in
Scholastic SCOPE® magazine, Vol. 46, No. 2, September 22, 1997.

ISBN 0-439-05717-5

15 14 13 12 23 06

Characters

Josh - a high school senior

Narrator - Josh recalling events

Mom - Josh's mother

Dad - Josh's father

Bo - head guide

Clint - TV producer

Kate - climber and medical student

Max - assistant guide

Tony - climber

Aya - young Sherpa guide

Mount Everest

Most airplanes don't even fly as high as the peaks of Mount Everest. Located on the Nepal-Tibet border, Everest is the tallest mountain in the world. For over a century, climbers have attempted to scale its icy summit. More than a hundred have died along the way.

In 1953, New Zealander Sir Edmund Hillary and his Nepalese guide, Tenzing Norgay, became the first climbers to reach the top. They carried bottled oxygen because breathing on Everest's summit is almost impossible.

The mountain is littered with the bottles of those who have followed. In the mid-1980s, amateur climbers began to pay guides to help them scale Everest. Many succeeded, but money guarantees nothing at the top of the world.

In the spring of 1996, 30 groups made the trek up Everest. Twelve people died. This play helps you imagine their terror.

Climbing Everest had always been my dream. I didn't know it would become a nightmare.

Act 1

Narrator: One night last winter, my life changed with a single phone call. Mom answered the phone. Her voice got cold, so I knew it was Dad.

Mom: I'll get Josh.

Narrator: My parents divorced years ago. Mom worked hard to support us. Meanwhile, Dad had become a TV producer. He made lots of money, but he didn't send much of it our way.

Josh: What's up, Dad?

Dad: You'll be graduating soon, and I've been thinking about your present.

Josh: I'm really into mountain climbing. How about some new gear?

Narrator: Mountain climbing was my thing. We lived in Oregon, and I'd climbed all the most extreme peaks in the West.

Dad: Here's a better idea. How about trekking up Everest with me and Clint, my business partner? Ever heard of Bo Collins? He's taking a group in a few months.

Narrator: I nearly choked. Climbing Everest had been my fantasy since I was ten years old. And as a guide, Collins was a legend.

Josh: Climb Everest? Are you serious? And with Bo Collins? But it costs $65,000 a person to go on his expeditions!

Dad: That's my department.

Josh: It sounds great, but Dad, are you sure you're in shape for this?

Dad: No sweat. I'm in training. Anyway, Bo might as well have paved a superhighway to the top.

Narrator: Mom grabbed the receiver.

Mom: Josh will not risk his life on Everest!

Narrator: She slammed down the phone.

Josh: Mom!

Mom: Do you know why Dad and I stopped climbing? Because our best friends died on Mount McKinley 20 years ago.

Josh: But Everest is my dream!

Mom: Everest is 29,000 feet high! You've got climbing skills, but you've never been anywhere *near* that altitude. You don't have any idea what it does to you.

Josh: Lots of people climb Everest. Business people. Politicians. Students. You don't have to be Superman to climb it anymore. You just need the right guide.

Mom: The answer is no.

Why do you think that Josh was so eager to climb Everest?

Hundreds of people had come to Base Camp to climb Everest. And the scene was not pretty.

Act 2

Narrator: I begged. I pleaded. Dad did, too. Finally, Mom gave in. Now, months later, I sat with Bo's team in a village called Lobuje, at 16,000 feet. The next day we'd hike to Everest Base Camp. From there, climbing would get tougher, trickier, and colder. We'd scramble through snow and over icy rock faces to Camps One through Four, each higher than the next. Finally, we'd reach the summit of Everest. The altitude already had me moving more slowly than usual.

Dad: Look at all of these groups! There must be 300 climbers trying for the top. Everest has become commercial.

Bo: Way *too* commercial.

Narrator: The camp looked like a garbage dump. There were empty oxygen bottles and other trash everywhere. It was really gross.

Kate: Everest is sacred to the Sherpas, but not sacred to these tourists, I guess.

Narrator: The Sherpas were the Nepali people who carried our supplies and set up camps for us. They handled altitude well because they lived in the mountains all year.

Max *(looking around)*: Half of these climbers are amateurs. They don't belong here.

Clint: I do. I tried Everest two years ago with a rival company. A storm kept us from the top. I'm counting on you to get me there this time.

Bo: We'll try.

Clint: You'd better do more than try! My partner and I produce network news. If you don't get us to the top, the world will know you're a bad bet.

Bo: That's enough. I'll go through this only once. Up here, Max, Aya, and I are the law. Everest is dangerous. By the time we get to Camp One, the oxygen will be so thin, we'll essentially begin dying. The trick is to get to the top and back while we're still alive. Many people don't. Why? Vision, endurance, and strength all get worse along the way. Your brain gets so slow, you don't think clearly. If we get good weather and you follow orders, we'll all get home safely. If not . . .

Everest was incredibly dangerous. The dead climbers along the trail were proof.

ACT 3

Narrator: We spent six weeks at Base Camp, which is at 17,600 feet. Every day, Bo led us higher to get us used to the altitude. Then he'd bring us back down again. The descents got pretty scary.

Clint: Be very careful. This icy log we're crossing is really shaky. And that crevasse below us looks like it's three miles deep.

Dad: Make one wrong move, and you're dead.

Narrator: We'd already passed two dead climbers. The first body really upset me. I tried to pretend the second one wasn't there.

Bo: Trust me, everyone. I'll get you down.

Narrator: Even when we rested, we felt sick and totally exhausted.

Kate: How are you holding up, Josh?

Narrator: I liked Kate. She was a medical student who'd spent two springs helping Bo at Base Camp. This year, he was letting her climb.

Josh: I'm used to climbing, but I'm not used to this altitude. I'm so tired I feel like I'm crawling. How about you?

Kate: I just can't digest anything, and I'm losing lots of weight.

Josh: You're still doing great.

Kate: Thanks, I guess.

Narrator: Just then, Nima, one of the Sherpas, passed by. He was coughing like crazy.

Kate: I'm worried about Nima's lungs, but he won't go back down to Lobuje.

Narrator: Kate was right to worry. By evening, Nima was delirious and coughing up blood.

Kate: His lungs are full of fluid. The other Sherpas will have to carry him down, or he'll die.

> How do you think Josh and his team felt when they saw the dead climbers?

We got sicker and sicker in the thin air. Was Everest even worth it?

Act 4

Narrator: That night, I talked to Dad and Clint.

Dad: You're spending lots of time with Kate.

Josh: She's nice, and she's smart.

Dad: Is that all?

Josh: She's pretty too.

Clint: It sounds like young love in bloom.

Josh: Cut it out. She's five years older than me. *(pause)* Is there any news about Nima?

Dad: The guys at Lobuje got a helicopter to take him to a hospital.

Clint: Luckily, we have plenty of other Sherpas.

Josh *(angry)*: We're talking about a man's life!

Dad: We know, son. But we can't do anything for Nima now. Let's just concentrate on the climb.

Clint: That's right. We're moving to Camp One

tomorrow. In no time, we'll be on top of the world!

Dad *(coughing)*: I just hope we'll be able to appreciate it. More and more, I think this trip isn't about climbing. It's about enduring pain.

Narrator: Days passed. We coughed. We shivered. We grew sicker in the thin air. Still, we kept climbing over ice and up incredibly steep, slick rock walls. We moved from Camp One to Camp Two to Camp Three. We were now at 24,000 feet.

Kate *(slurring)*: Josh, how are you managing?

Josh: When we were climbing that last rock face, I blacked out for a while. And you don't sound so good yourself.

Kate: My tongue's swollen.

Josh: You know, Kate, Everest was my dream. Now I wonder if it's worth it. It's not like I expected. That thing with Nima upset me. And seeing those dead climbers . . .

Kate: Me, too.

We started for the summit before dawn. Would we make it to the top?

ACT 5

Narrator: The time had come. It was just before dawn. We were going for the summit.

Bo: Okay, everyone, if you're not at the top by two o'clock, turn around. Otherwise you'll get caught in the dark and never get back.

Clint: Collins, if I don't make the summit, I'll expose your little company on national news.

Narrator: I could tell that Clint's threats were making Bo nervous. Still, Bo tried to ignore him.

Bo: Everybody has oxygen, right? Without it, you can't think. You could walk right off a cliff.

Dad: We're ready.

Bo: If you need help, call me or Max. Aya will be down tending camp.

Narrator: We began the final climb. I was the first to reach the top. Dad was right behind me.

Dad: Do you believe it? We made it to the top.

Josh: All my life I've dreamed of this. Now I'm so tired that all I want is to get back down.

Dad: Me, too. It's the weirdest thing.

Narrator: We stood on the summit for a few minutes. Then we took some pictures. We started down, and soon we ran into Max, Kate, and Tony.

Dad: Where's Clint?

Max: He's behind us. He's struggling, but don't worry. Bo will get him up here.

Narrator: Dad and I hiked back to the summit with the others for a group photo. At two, we all started down. At two-thirty, we passed Bo and Clint still climbing up.

Max: It's past two. Turn around!

Clint: No way! I missed the summit last time!

Bo: We'll be okay. They predicted a storm, but the weather's holding.

Max: Bo . . .

Bo: You heard me. Just take the others down.

Narrator: An hour later, a blizzard started. The air was so white we couldn't see a thing.

We were lost. We felt like we were freezing to death. And we probably were. . . .

Act 6

Narrator: We stumbled around for hours. We could barely see anything. Then it got dark.

Max *(confused)*: The camp should be, uh, somwhere down there.

Kate: We need lamps and oxygen. I feel like . . .

Tony: Like you're losing your mind? Freezing to death? You are. We all are!

Max: Stomp your feet! Keep moving. It will keep you alive.

Narrator: We were terrified. We were freezing. We knew we were near death. We figured we were probably close to our camp, but we were too groggy to find the path.

Max: Huddle behind this boulder. Get some shelter from the wind.

Narrator: We stood behind the rock. We couldn't

even see each other. Then, a miracle happened. A lamp shone through the snow. Aya had found us.

Aya: Follow us. We'll get you back to camp.

Narrator: I looked, but I didn't see Kate and Tony. They must have passed out in the snow.

Josh: Kate! Tony!

Narrator: No one answered. Then Aya's lamp suddenly flickered out.

Aya: The light's out. We have to start back before we lose our bearings.

Josh: We can't leave Kate and Tony!

Max: Aya is right. We can't risk losing our way. There's nothing we can do for them now. We'll come back in the morning—when we can see.

Narrator: I didn't want to leave, but I had to. Dad, Max, Aya, and I struggled back to camp.

Did Josh and the group do the right thing leaving Kate and Tony behind?

Could we find Kate and Tony? Would they still be alive? I could only hope.

Act 7

Narrator: The next day, the blizzard kept raging. Still, we dragged ourselves out. We finally found Kate and Tony buried in the snow.

Josh: Are they dead?

Aya: No, but they're unconscious and frostbitten. They might as well be dead. There's nothing we can do for them.

Josh: Don't say that!

Max: It's the truth, Josh.

Josh: Can't we drag them back to the tents?

Dad: We can barely walk. Dragging them is not an option. We'd die too.

Josh: Max? These are your clients!

Max: I have to save the ones who have a chance.

Narrator: Tears froze on my face. Max turned

away. He spoke by radio to Bo. The blizzard had trapped him near the top of the mountain.

Max: How are you? How's Clint?

Bo *(slurring)*: Clint is . . . dead.

Narrator: Dad's face crumpled.

Max: What about you?

Bo: I'm too frostbitten to move. Can't think. Can someone come get me?

Max: The blizzard would blow us off the trail. Can you hang in there?

Bo: I'll try.

Narrator: All around, people were dead or dying. I didn't know I could feel as bad as I did.

I couldn't believe it. A figure stumbled toward us, black with frostbite.

Act 8

Narrator: The blizzard stopped the next day. We were too sick to get down the mountain on our own. Other climbers with extra oxygen came up for us. Then Aya pointed toward a figure a few feet away.

Aya: Look!

Narrator: Tony, his face blackened by frostbite, shuffled toward us.

Josh: You're alive!

Tony *(slurred)*: I woke up, wanted to live.

Josh: Maybe Kate's alive too!

Narrator: I went back to where we'd left her. She was dead. I couldn't stop crying. I piled little rocks on her body to cover her. I didn't want Kate to be just another body on the side of the trail. When I finished, I saw that Dad had followed me.

Josh: Maybe we could have saved her.

Dad: We made the best decision we could. We didn't have a choice.

Josh: You didn't care! None of you! Tony is alive. If we'd tried harder, maybe Kate would be, too.

Dad: More likely, we'd be dead along with her.

Narrator: Dad, Tony, Max, Aya, and I eventually made it down the mountain, although Tony lost both feet to frostbite. Clint, Bo, and Kate are gone forever. In the end, Nima died too. I'll never stop thinking about them, especially Kate. Everest will always haunt me. It also taught me the value of human life. Life is too short, I say now. Help people who need it. Do what you can. You only get one chance.